Tell and Show™ Books are designed to foster imagination, creativity, and just plain fun. Illustrating a story can help young children understand and remember what the story is about. And an older child may enjoy illustrating the book for a younger one.

Illustrations can be complex or simple. **Pencils, color pencils,** and **crayons** work well, or pens that don't smear or soak through the page.

```
TEST
PENS
HERE
```

One Way To Use This Book

1. Don't draw yet. First, read the whole story, or listen as someone else reads it. Picture in your mind what's happening in the story.

2. Go back and read the first page of the story again. Then **draw a picture** in the blank space on the facing page.

3. Read until you get to the next blank page, and **make another picture.** Keep going until all the blank pages have pictures.

4. On the cover, **write your name where it says "illustrations by"** (a permanent marker works well on the cover). If others helped draw, add their names also. Fill in the "illustrations by" oval on the title page, too, and add to the dedication page if you like.

Enjoy your book! Share it with friends.

Ann Marie, The Noisiest Kid in the Class is also available as a black-and-white **PDF edition**, for printing on standard 8.5 x 11-inch paper. Each 11-inch-wide page has text on the left and space for drawing on the right. You can print or photocopy the whole PDF or individual pages, as many times as you need. If you'd like to have the PDF edition, email us to request it at:

tellandshow@daytonpublishing.com

Ann Marie, the Noisiest Kid in the Class

A Tell and Show™ Book

story by
Lindy Brown

illustrations by

Copyright © 2013 by Lindy Brown
All rights reserved

No part of this book may be used or reproduced in any manner without written permission from the publisher, except brief excerpts used in the context of a review.

Tell and Show™ edition

Printed and bound in USA

Dayton Publishing LLC
Solana Beach, CA 92075
858-254-2959
publisher@daytonpublishing.com

ISBN-13: 978-0-9893290-1-9

Tell and Show™ Books is an imprint of Dayton Publishing.

With thanks to all who helped,
and special thanks to
Savanna and Camille,
Mary and Sheila,
Betsy, Bobbie, Jenni, and Gage

— *Lindy Brown*

On Monday morning Ann Marie clattered down the hall of Lynnbrook School and hurried into Mrs. Rothmann's classroom.

"Hi, Ann Marie!" said Mrs. Rothmann. "Try not to bang the door," she reminded her.

Uh-oh . . .

"Sorry, Mrs. Rothmann!"

Ann Marie shrugged off her backpack and dropped it beside her desk:

THUD.

The bell rang, and the school day began.

"Good morning, everyone!" said Mrs. Rothmann. "It's so nice to see you."

The school day starts.

During math Ann Marie worked hard. She didn't even notice she was tapping her pencil:

Mrs. Rothmann raised her eyebrows.

During silent reading Ann Marie's knees bounced her desk up and down.

thunk, thunk, thunk, thunk

"Ann Marie, *please!*" said Mrs. Rothmann.

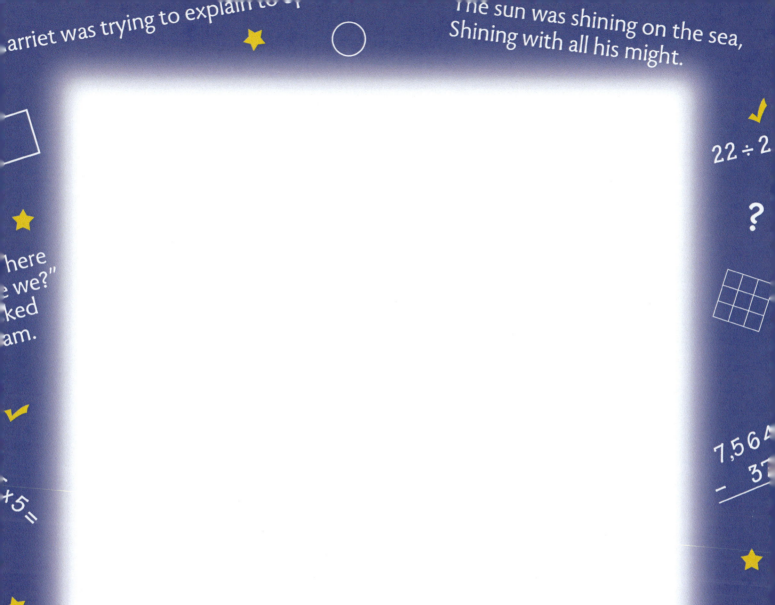

Doing school work

During spelling Ann Marie practiced rocking her chair back and forth on its two back legs. She was balancing *perfectly* — but then she leaned back a little too far.

Uh-oh . . .

The chair tipped and slid out from under her!

CRASH!

"ANN MARIE!" Mrs. Rothmann's voice was much louder than usual.

"I'm okay, Mrs. Rothmann!" Ann Marie said. She picked herself up and straightened her chair.

As the spelling lesson went on, other kids tried balancing their chairs on two legs also. No one else tipped over, but Suzellen and Carlos almost did.

After lunch Mrs. Rothmann read to the class from a story book, as she did every day. Ann Marie oh-so-quietly reached into her backpack and oh-so-carefully took out the ten acorns she had collected on a hike with her dad. She planned to silently line them up on her desk, from smallest to biggest, while she listened to the story and thought up a new knock-knock joke.

But two of the acorns slipped through her fingers! And when she grabbed for those, the other acorns escaped too!

Uh-oh . . .

The acorns bounced on her desk.

click! click! click! click! click!
click! click! click! click! click!

Then they bounced onto the floor.

**CLACK! CLACK! CLACK! CLACK!
CLACK! CLACK! CLACK!
CLACK! CLACK!
CLACK!**

Then they bounced again and rolled away in all directions.

Alice was getting very tired of sitting by her sister on the bank, and of having nothing to do. ... suddenly, thump! thump! down she came upon a heap of sticks and dry leaves, and the fall was over. ... "How doth the little crocodile improve his shining tail, and pours the waters of the Nile on every golden scale!" ... It was high time to go, for the pool was getting quite crowded with the birds and animals that had fallen into it.

Acorns!

"ANN MARIE!" Mrs. Rothmann's voice rang out. ***"Bring me those acorns right now!"***

Ann Marie gathered up her acorns, inched over to Mrs. Rothmann's desk, and handed them over. Mrs. Rothmann put them into her top desk drawer and shut it.

"Come and see me after school," she said, "and I'll give them back to you."

Whew . . . thank goodness!

Mrs. Rothmann closed the story book without finishing the chapter. "Class, I think we need some fresh air and exercise," she said. "Let's take a walk in the woods."

The class filed out the back door of the school into the sunshine. They bounded across the playground. Then they lined up behind Mrs. Rothmann and strolled along the path into the woods. They looked at the beautiful yellow, red, and brown autumn leaves and smelled the autumn air.

Ann Marie stopped beside a small fallen log.

"Let's see who's under here," she said. She carefully rolled the log over. Roly-poly bugs, earthworms, and even a salamander wriggled on the cool, moist dirt underneath.

"Look at that!" said Zorah.

"Wow!" said Tyler.

Ann Marie gently rolled the log back into place. She was careful not to squash the animals.

As the class moved on, they stopped now and then so Mrs. Rothmann or Ann Marie or one of the other kids could roll over another log or a rock. Sometimes they found animals underneath, and sometimes they didn't.

"It's a treasure hunt!" said Maxine.

a roly-poly isopod (pronounced "eye-so-pod")

earthworms

a salamander

Looking under logs and rocks

As they walked farther, Ann Marie saw a small yellowish object hanging down from a low branch.

"Look!" she said.

The class gathered around. At first they thought the object was a rolled-up leaf. But when they looked more closely, they could see it wasn't a leaf at all.

"A caterpillar attached itself to the branch and then turned into this chrysalis," Ann Marie said. "Someday a butterfly will come out."

The class looked from the chrysalis to Ann Marie and back to the chrysalis.

"It's truly amazing, isn't it?" said Mrs. Rothmann.

caterpillar

**chrysalis
(pronounced
"kriss-uh-liss")**

butterfly

Finding a chrysalis

A few steps farther on, Ann Marie pointed high overhead. "See that bunch of sticks way up there in that tree?"

Everyone looked up.

"It's a hawks' nest," said Ann Marie. "After the parents hatched their eggs and raised their babies, the whole family flew away. But the parents might come back next year and use the same nest again."

"Imagine a family of hawks living there," said Mrs. Rothmann. "Isn't it interesting? Some kinds of birds fix up their nests and use them again and again, but other species build a new nest every spring."

an empty nest

hawks in flight

The hawks' nest

Looking down at the bottom of the hawks'-nest tree, Ann Marie spotted a hole.

"Mice or rabbits might live here," she said. The other kids came closer to have a look.

"Or maybe a harmless little garter snake," said Ann Marie. Some of the kids jumped back.

"My goodness, it's getting late!" said Mrs. Rothmann before they could go too far. "What a lovely walk we've had. But we'd better go back now. Let's line up!"

Suddenly Maxine grabbed Mrs. Rothmann's hand. "I think I heard a bear..."

Erik gasped, "I heard it, too!"

"It's right over there!" Penelope trembled. She hid behind Ann Marie.

Is there a bear?

"I'm sure there aren't any bears in these woods," said Mrs. Rothmann. "Anyway, most bears are shy around people. They'll usually run away if they hear you coming. So if ever you think there might be a bear around, it's a good idea to . . ."

"MAKE SOME NOISE!" shouted Ann Marie.

She picked up two sticks and dashed to the front of the line. Maxine let go of Mrs. Rothmann's hand to take the stick Ann Marie held out to her.

"If there *are* any bears around, tapping with these sticks will let them know we're coming," Ann Marie said.

"Let's make some noise!"

Ann Marie and Maxine tapped the tree trunks beside the path as they walked — not hard enough to hurt the trees, just hard enough to make a sharp

TAP! TAP! TAP! TAP!

As she tapped, Ann Marie also stomped through the fallen leaves on the path.

STOMP! CRACKLE! STOMP! CRACKLE!

Soon the others were doing it too, stomping and laughing and having a great time.

STOMP! CRACKLE! STOMP! CRACKLE! TAP!

They told knock-knock jokes and sang made-up songs — loudly. And they got all the way back to the school without seeing a single bear.

Heading back to school

When the school's-out bell rang, Mrs. Rothmann said, "Good-bye, children. See you all tomorrow!"

Everyone said good-bye and hurried out the door — except Ann Marie. She picked up her backpack and headed over to Mrs. Rothmann's desk.

Mrs. Rothmann handed over the acorns in a small paper bag. "Thank you for showing us those wonderful things in the woods today, Ann Marie," she said. "And thanks for your help with the bear scare. You and I know there aren't any bears in those woods, but the other children weren't so sure. You were a big help. On your way now!"

"Okay, Mrs. Rothmann. See you tomorrow!"

As Ann Marie hurried out of the room, her backpack bumped against the door:

THWACK!

And the door slammed behind her.

Good-bye until tomorrow!

a **TIP** *from an artist*

Color Magic

"To me, color has always seemed magical," says artist Ed Roxburgh. "My Great Uncle Allan painted beautiful landscapes in oils. One day when I was about 10 years old, he showed me this really neat trick. If we stare at a particular color for a while and then look at an empty white space, we see that same shape but in a different color."

Try it out. Stare at the **x** in the center of the red square at the right for about 30 seconds. Then look at the **x** in the empty white space next to the square. What do you see?

Most people will see a greenish-blue square; another name for this color is *cyan*. The cyan square is an illusion called an *afterimage*. Here's why it happens: Red and cyan are *complementary colors* of light, a pair of colors that combine to make white light. Here's another way to look at it: If you start with white light and take away the red, what's left is the complementary color, cyan.

Our eyes have color *receptors* that report to the brain how much of each color of light is coming into the eye. The light coming into the eye from the blank page is white. But in the area of each eye that has been staring at the red square, the red-reporting parts of the receptors are temporarily "tired out." Until they recover (in just a minute or so), they can't report red to the brain very well. The cyan-reporting parts are working just fine, though. With little or no red being reported from the square shape, the brain "sees" a cyan square.

A related illusion can happen at the edges of a color. For instance, yellow clouds painted on a pale gray sky can appear to have bluish or purplish edges, even though no blue or purple paint was used.

"To me, it's magic," says Ed, who works with color illusions every day in his painting.

An Artist's Story

Ed Roxburgh is glad he chose a career he can enjoy all his life. Besides his own landscape paintings, Ed has painted scenery for plays, operas, TV series, movies — even haunted houses. He also paints murals in hotels and restaurants. And he illustrates children's books.

Ed has always loved to draw and paint. When he got into some trouble and had to change middle schools, he left his "bad kid" identity behind, but took his art with him. His classmates liked to watch him draw, and that helped him fit in at the new school. His art teacher asked Ed if she could enter his work in a contest. When he first saw his winning artwork printed in a national magazine, "it was a really pleasant feeling," Ed says. "I started to understand that even if I was feeling frustrated or alienated, I'd be okay. I'd just paint — just make my own 'happy.' "

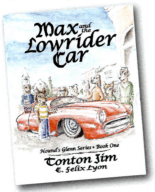 

When he illustrates children's books, Ed Roxburgh goes by the name E. Felix Lyon. Here "Felix" paints the cover illustration for *Max and the Lowrider Car*, the first book in the *Hound's Glenn* series, written by Tonton Jim. Ed has developed a way to illustrate that combines pencil sketching, computer technology, and watercolor. He draws in black pencil on any white paper, then scans the finished pencil drawing and uses a computer program to clean up any eraser smudges or other unwanted marks. Next the drawing is printed in permanent black on watercolor paper, and Ed can paint with watercolors to bring the picture to life. If he decides he wants to make big changes to the painting, he can make another print and start over with the watercolors.

Made in the USA
Monee, IL
04 April 2023

30792008R00019